Into the Same Sound Twice

Into the Same Sound Twice

Zakia Carpenter-Hall

Seren is the book imprint of
Poetry Wales Press Ltd.
Suite 6, 4 Derwen Road, Bridgend, Wales, CF31 1LH
www.serenbooks.com
facebook.com/SerenBooks
twitter@SerenBooks

The right of Zakia Carpenter-Hall to be identified as
the author of this work has been asserted in accordance
with the Copyright, Designs and Patents Act, 1988.

© Zakia Carpenter-Hall, 2023

ISBN: 978-1-78172-705-8

A CIP record for this title is available from the British Library.

The publisher acknowledges the financial assistance of the Books Council of Wales.

Cover artwork: Angelique Stephenson

Printed in Bembo by 4Edge Ltd, Hockley

Contents

Shakespeare Honours My Grandmother   7
Big Talk   8
Tree Art   9
Flesh & Tree   10
The Gold Price   12
Dust   13
Into the Same Sound Twice   14
The Earth-Eating Fire   15
Capaea Nemoralis   19
Animal Eden   20
The Pitch   21
Twelve Seconds of Film   22
Chasing Rainbows   26
What is the Heart of a River   28
She Found God in Herself and She Loved Her Fiercely   31
&   32
Notes   34
Acknowledgements   35

'Time… is neither linear nor circular. It's an entanglement.'
~ *Chris Abani*

Shakespeare Honours My Grandmother

On the day Grandma Ruth will be buried,
actors as pallbearers carry the likeness
of a body wrapped in white cloth,
held together with twine. The priest,

like those in Coptic churches, holds
a gold censer wafting frankincense,
known for its sweetness. The actress'
likeness is placed into a gravesite onstage

which happens to be under the thrones
of Kings and moves on an axis. Grandma's
funeral, four thousand miles away, has begun,
my only regret is that I am late to admission.

The theatre is so dark the usher can't see
where I am supposed to sit. She doesn't know
I am the granddaughter of the deceased,
but places me closer to the burial site,

nearer to those who grieve. I can touch
the procession, hum words to the funeral song.
I know this is not how Grandma Ruth's funeral
will go, her body carried from the highest point

to the lowest. There may be some African prints
but few bright colours, and no priest. I can see
the play, but also my grandmother's ancestral home –
how they welcome her today with ritual and song.

Big Talk

'when the mystics speak of worlds beyond scent and colour,
the common man […] cannot grasp their reality.'
~ Rumi, translated by Maryam Mafi and Azima Melita Kolin

Cosmologists say, 'If the sun was a door,
Earth would be the size of a dime.'
And I try to envision the vastness that I love –
a sun-door through which Earth could enter.

Carlo Rovelli uses the analogy of a kiss.
He asks, 'Where is the kiss now?' So I follow
the event through a series of synapses,
the sensations both on and below my skin

until what's left is the remembered kiss. The past
being carried by light is like film developed
in a dark room. Space isn't distinct from matter,
it bends like a seashell around the gravity of planets.

We're living in a universe that doesn't make sense
when trying to approach it through the senses.

Tree Art

It had been such a long time, I was surprised by how gently my mother made my hair, asking if she should split the rows, my locs beginning to intertwine. As if using a miniature rake of a Japanese garden, she attended to the grove of my hair – so that it barely registered as touch. I couldn't imagine that she was doing it right, what with the absence of pain and discomfort, but she did, ordering and reordering, twisting my roots so they wouldn't come loose and fastening them next to each other with silver clips for added strength, so they could dry.

She says everything is an experiment, and she has some trees that can be manicured into different shapes; she likes the square staircase upwards, the gradually widening circles from tip to base. She says she has some foliage to practice on, with her newly gentle hands. Or maybe I had simply forgotten what my mother's hands and fingers in my hair had felt like. She had never done my locs before, I had to show her how to grasp the new growth and then palm roll it. My mom is more familiar with two-strand twists, braids, Nubian knots, the iconic Afro or natural, like leafy trellises opening towards sunlight.

I almost expect my hair to blossom and grow Pyrus communis fruits, pears being a type of rose, or at least descended from them. I once decorated my French braid with fabric flowers all along the crisscross lattice. I was beginning to think my hair was the length of an entire afternoon. But my hair was like the basil plant whose leaves had begun to dry out and curl inward – once watered, it surprised us all and flowered.

Flesh & Tree

After '16th Century Ivory Salt Cellar, Sierra Leone'

This conversation piece made of ivory:
a bowl with three raised relief crocodiles
roaming the circumference, atop half a dozen

curved supports in herringbone, beading
and zigzag motifs, between six perched parrots; two
fleur-de-lys on either side of the canonical base.

      I could imagine the salt cellar morphing
      into a djembe drum, a taut hide of calf skin
      pulled over its rim, base and internal chamber
      resonant with new music, clinks of hail:
      small kernels can look like granules of salt.

Where I grew up there were snow storms
and West African dance classes. Ice falling
from the sky like fruit, hail the size of lemons or limes.

We could take the salt cellar's curved supports
and squeeze them like the netting on a calabash,
every design feature subservient to the music.

      How do you play an instrument you've inherited
      but weren't taught? What will I conjure?
      Delight has so many unknown nodes. Where
      do I place my hands? This is not a choice between
      the zest of powerful flavours or sultry rhythms.

The drum isn't an ordinary medium. It's made
from flesh and tree, plant and animal.
One needs to be alive to play it, an art

of skin to skin. Tension strings, to change
pitch and depth of sound, shell like a chalice,
a hieroglyph of symbols carved along the foot.

Fingers will callous with regular use.
Forearms will hurt and then swell,
and ache some more as muscles
break down in order to regrow,
new cells funnel in to fill gaps.

Some drummers close their eyes and sing
over great distances: the space between
two bodies or points of pleasure.

One needs strength to play this instrument
and an impeccable sense of timing. A djembe
left open is like cupped hands awaiting fuel.

The Gold Price

'The asking price for everything was a nugget of gold, which no one had.'
~ Clarissa Pinkola Estés, 'Jack and The Beanstalk'

My mother can turn false golds green,
so here's the test: my father, as trusting
as Jack, brings home some metal alloy

gleaming like a love that is so pure,
it's suspect. And neither my mother
nor I believe it could be real, and so

we test it. First for its story, which
sounds too much like a fable. Next,
for costs: a fourth of his stimulus check.

I worry about Jack, who keeps buying gold
to bestow his love, with everyone around him
disbelieving; we say that even the 18 karat

engraving could be forged. My mother
immerses this token of love in rubbing alcohol,
dabs it dry, wears it all night. When it survives,

she scrapes the exterior, tests its pliancy,
supplies a magnet to see whether the necklace
will be drawn towards it, and later watches

a silent video of a ring held suspended
in fire for a long time, and my mother seems
unsure whether it was the colour of the flame,

the consistency of the metal, the temperature
of the fire, or that the ring did not melt,
which was the true indication of its worth.

12

Dust

I heard – out of nowhere – the resonant moans of a cello, and perhaps this was in response to hitting a certain pitch of feeling, a film where a couple takes a road trip and things begin to fall apart, that's when the cello sounded. I can't think in unknown music. But the washing machine provided an ambient sound and I was able to pick up on a signal not emitted from the neighbours. The theme music for stubborn gladness or a sweet but bitter need, a home that can't be returned to convened in my living room playing tenors of ache that I could not name, but had found an audience in me. I pressed my ear to the walls to find out if the noise level grew. Could I be the instrument? I checked the volume on all my devices. The resonance of those low levels of longing and mourning continued to play, though I could not translate it. I am not a musician. The melody paused in time with the washing machine as if to take a breath. I thought about people who claim to record the dead and say ghosts prefer to speak over a running faucet or radio wave static, as though a sharp white background is a kind of net. Then enter French horns in a casual flutter, everything taking its time, and talking at once, a movement. When the washer stopped, so did the jazz.

Into the Same Sound Twice

As a child, I mixed up the words musician
and magician. I couldn't be sure which one
relied on magic, which was mostly preparation.
Which artist makes something appear from nothing,
who carries instruments, sculpts emotions,
or has mastered misdirection? Are dancers
magicians or musicians? I play close, I *pay* close
attention to their music, no – their muscle isolations,
transitions between stillness and motion, between
gestures: crisp definition, rough, raw, or sequenced
as the splicing of frames in a film – seams invisible.
I wanted to know about magicians, so I watched
Black Thought freestyle for ten minutes. I'm thinking
of David Blaine when he pushed a solid metal rod
through his arm, then his hand, both times missing
all blood vessels and arteries; he didn't bleed. It got me
thinking, Does a lyrical emcee dance or perform magic?
When the lyricist starts rocking to the momentum
of his words, or spitting according to the rhythm
like he's charting a course with his body, is it intuition
which guides and fills the sails of his lungs
across the sea of a looped sound sample? As he creates
his own weather, not the rhythm but the climate,
mirror neurons firing, head nods flicker through
the crowd in agreement. The lyricist 'dances'.
This 'dance' is in his head and in his body, colours
begin to be elicited by music, hues of blues and purples.
I fall into it, lose track of time, my relationship
to sound deepens. His lyricism slippery, eel-like. Safety
is a slick business. The audience endeavours not to drown
in the undertow of a current that pulls us beneath it,
baritone but siren-like, as it calls us to disembark
and wade in something we're not ready to be freed of,
the song is a good net, we the sweet captives
can feel a tingling sensation in our toes
and limbic systems, our vagus nerves electric
as a singer thunders, *And I dared to leave* amidst ripples
of reverberating bass. We can't turn away; we sheep.

The Earth-Eating Fire

'They said if we suppress all these fires, we end light burning, we will have great new forests. And we did – we had so much great new forest that we created a problem.'
~ Stephen Pyne, fire historian

Oya's dress of vapour hangs in the air
a texture of haunting, a series of negatives,
transparencies, x-rays. we see through an oak's
missing heartwood, ghost of coiled roots
upturned, exposed, releasing a pantheon of spirits,
the whole forest spins, as if on display.

open pinecones gummed in resin,
sink them into soft soil, spell of effluvium,
fumigate, smoke – be the cure.
separate good fire from wild,
peel back brambles layer by layer.
may running waters reach our interior
with the help of your embers.

the fire-fearful,
fear flames will jump holding lines –
(run, fly, shape-shift) as they sometimes do
into communities
fear fire cannot be ~~controlled~~ conned
– an escaped fire (cause for alarm)
burning to distinguish good fire from wicked
see fire as funeral, as pyre,
as a spreading crematorium.

Anomaly of Wind

SssssSSSSssssshhhhhHHhHHShShshshshshshshshshshshshhhh
WhhoooooooowhhhhoooooooooooooooooThhhhhhhhhhsssssssssss
Hisssssssssssssssswwwwwwwwwwwwwoooooooooooooooooooooo
HeeeeeehheeecceeeeeeeeeeeeeeeeeSsssssssssssssssssheeeeeeeeeee

in the blazing wildfires, you wonder what sounds the trees made as they
burned.

in a flash, a prickly feeling,
everything can change,
volatile as a compound
that refuses stasis, steals
protons and electrons
from passersby to become
some other form.

joy can come with mourning,
for a while it was difficult to celebrate
the hardest thing that's happened.
i mourned but the joy did not come.
i think of how best to commemorate this pruning.

the god who sees problems
as opportunities to dance, was showing me
beauty – or the edge of my suffering
is exquisite, a prescribed burn, or that pain
is a circle with vegetation along
inner and outer rings. i listened
for the lyricism in crackling,
the artistry in chewing through dry matter,
breaking down the fourth wall of thorns.

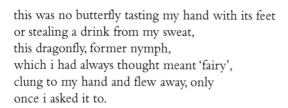

this was no butterfly tasting my hand with its feet
or stealing a drink from my sweat,
this dragonfly, former nymph,
which i had always thought meant 'fairy',
clung to my hand and flew away, only
once i asked it to.

anti-logging protestors
plant themselves in cement
using an iron seed
called 'sleeping dragon', or
wedge themselves
in tripod barricades
made from felled trees,
or nest in branches,
or block roads
made for lorries
to protect the old groves,
trees half the age of Gilgamesh.

i named you each month that you remained:
habitat, medicine, food, health, dense woods, canopy, respite, shade.

this heat will devour   undergrowth   lap tree moss
blister hazel stalks   *coax*   brave new shoots   for newborns'
wicker baskets   caps   &   *entice*
                                            acorns
                                                to
                                                    fall.

```
          heat will broil
              rain guzzling
                  invasive plants
                      so chilled water
                      streams through
              flames' charred wake,
          down into watershed
and Klamath river nourishing the salmon.

          soon bear grass
              huckleberries reaching
                  for water
              overrun by scotch brook,
                  fir trees
          thickets of blackberries
          animals will travel here
          for a dip in ash baths'
                  cooling
              natural antiseptic.
```

but this fire will not cure the climate.

prescription: eight parts dead leaf. one part sun. three parts ozone
charged firmament. six parts still undisturbed air.

on the eve
of an afternoon,
in a little clearing,
below an amber sun
and a canopy of pines,
the cultural burn begins.

Capaea Nemoralis

Take a day it was supposed to rain but didn't. Use this mis-forecast or false prophecy to pull bindweed up from soil you didn't realise was soft and obliging. Don't linger too long on those of your forebears bred [by barbarians] to make light work of the Earth. Sense goosefoot almost disintegrate in your hands. This continent, with different coordinates in spacetime, your strength grows with each pile of plant flesh, fibre and root carried to its destination of disposal. Hard work is good for mental health [you've heard this somewhere haven't you?]. Though you didn't mean to squash a grove snail underneath the sole of your industrious shoe, for capaea nemoralis it was the crushing weight of dark matter. The wild has its own tactics. If you begin to itch, remember just about everything trying to survive has teeth; pick scattered seeds, spiralled like tiny pinwheel galaxies, from the sleeve of your sweater. Your ancestors would've had less protection from burrs, thorns and heat. Search your skin for environmental irritations, anything that might cause an angry rash to occur. Bees circumnavigate your head in protest of the mess you've made of their flowers. Try to stop the line of thinking that demands you earn your keep: be a mogul, be a Josephine of all trades, *make that shit you do so good it seems to glitter,* so you may keep your life / style to which you've grown accustomed. When the fog of your mood has lifted, and you've learned that your body doesn't want to be a machine so much as an instrument, don't think of food as the reward. Smile in a wry half-gleam when you realise the hardest working are the ones most often accused of sloth. In a cosmos ninety-three billion light years wide and expanding, you are not a fixed star in anybody's sky.

19

Animal Eden

It was the year of the viral video,
nature coming out of hiding.
We were supposed to believe
that within weeks, animal lives
had overwritten us with their joy
and reckless abandon, instincts
alerting them like radio waves
signalling through the ether that humans
were under quarantine and no one
knew how long. Elephants
who'd eaten *Earth knows what*,
forgot about – the human dangers,
perhaps consumed themselves
into a stupor of corn wine and laid out
in cultivated fields of tea leaves.
I hate to anthropomorphize,
but were those smiles that I saw on all
of their faces? With the predators
of the world gone gone – vanished –
the prey had reached an Earthly nirvana,
and it was heaven! Heaven on Earth!
Heaven at last! And some of us humans,
from the vantage point of our dark screens,
felt so good for having seen it.

The Pitch

Instead of words, rocaille beads pour from my
mouth and all the garments I've presented
have been held together with a glue gun
applied to the seams. Ms. Fashion Exec says,
How do you plan to make money?, as the
carpet begins to unspool because that too was
somehow made by me, flecks of paint peel off
the walls and swirl around the room. I am as
silent as snowfall, but I show them diamonds
made of paper, shoes constructed solely in felt.
One interviewer asks whether or not this is a
joke. This is not a business, the panel says, as
the room fills up with my attempts – like the
enchanted broom in *Fantasia* which kept going
back to bring forth buckets of water long past
there being a need – drawings I drew, dance
choreography. It's too much, they say, all this
longing and striving. A gale comes in of the
same force that's beating against my lungs, as if
someone's opened windows on the 100th floor
of a skyscraper, this ledge of fashion, and this
gust eats at the panel's notes. The judges still try
to get their questions to me by courier, their
clothes billow away from their bodies. What
would you do if you had the money?, they ask.
I tell them there would be more of me, and I
would be gesticulating like a conductor in the
centre of it all. Waves of sound and light crash
at my feet. Building works commence next
door and it sounds as though the workers are
trying to break into the room with chisels. The
panel take out their Louis Vuitton hard hats
and persist, like this is just another wardrobe
malfunction. And the room begins to glow
white-hot.

Twelve Seconds of Film

When the water rose
in mid-air as if to form

a kind of liquid lace,
I was mesmerized

that something so fluid, even
through the use of CGI,

could be contained. Rivers
are routes, guides, navigation;

I could feel the room fill
with liquid. The mind

is like that: holding
a fragile irrecoverable thing

suspended, then forging
a path to get there,

in the surrealist way. What's true
is I hungered for such

occurrences in daily life,
to get so deep into my studies

that forests would become
moving labyrinths around me.

What I wanted was perpetual
autumn and to walk, no

glide up the trunks of trees,
to try on a new physics. What I asked

once was, *If there was another
place to go, would you leave?*

What I meant was: such a place
where the ordinary rules

of motion wouldn't apply.
My guess is that one would

have to go far out, into the deep
woods of space, so far as to make

any return impossible, farther still,
to hear space's own singular heartbeat,

as though all that void,
vacuum, cosmos could

after all turn out to be a body
on a multiverse-sized scale.

It was something about
the water having risen,

the actors placed in the midst
of standing waves, something

about this also being a miracle
of technology and storytelling,

a key plot point – the water –
would fall, wouldn't it? Because

eventually there's gravity
pulling all of our thoughts

and ideas to the ground
making us contend with

today. The characters had
to walk the map, one could say

they had to walk on water. What
was it? Their world turned

upside down, two different mazes
on alternate sides, one silver marble

to thread through them? They didn't
know water had this function, less

transparent than it is reflective?
When a vessel carrying water breaks,

for a moment water retains its shape
like the formation of stratus before rain.

Is that it? And in the film,
the water was swirling around

the actors' heads like clouds. I
needed some images from a different

cultural lexicon. Water
as liquid, particle, wave, alive

in its swirls, as magical as
watching acrylic move on canvas,

enlivening all things – as if
paint could keep its range

of motion continuing to rivulet,
blossom secondary and tertiary colours

as it went, everything making
more sense when in motion

and ceasing to mean when fixed.
The water had just enough

movement in it to remain relevant,
to spark my curiosity – it idled there –

a new thought or way of knowing,
a novel being coming into view,

before falling to the floor, everyone
in the room enthralled with what it means,

what to do next, deciphering
its calligraphy. I was consumed

with water being a language
and quite possibly *the language*,

my language for thought, my need
for the cascading fountain

of happenings down the sometimes
staircase, sometimes scaffold of the line,

its contour. I pour my thinking
down them. Imagine water

maintaining its shape for a moment;
see currents like tendons

stretched across bone. I could see
all of the colours, each one a thread

or a band of light, the nuances of blues
caught up in a stream of lights and darks.

Chasing Rainbows

Someone has changed their name to Chasing Rainbows. I overheard this outside my window from passersby discussing their friend who had changed his name. Of course I thought of all the cliché and glitter I could muster, fairies and unicorns and pixie dust, and if I knew this friend how I would address him, encourage him, admonish him, always using his full name. Good luck, Chasing Rainbows! Terrific job, Chasing Rainbows! ¡O qué lastima, Chasing Rainbows!, if he spoke Spanish. And it might be as though he was always on the job – mission and mantra within the name – of searching for beautiful ephemera but never grasping it, light refracting in the prism of raindrops and reflecting across the sky.

I think of that point in childhood when we're inclined to search for the invisible – perhaps it never leaves us. I once wondered whether I could fly, but tested this above the immense cushion of a mattress. Can't you see that the heart-filled canopy I grew out of, he kept, my love for sparkly, frilly, chiming, enchanting, spectacular things.

Chasing Rainbows loves too sweet icing and chocolate cake, glitter and glitz, fashion forward tutus and light-up wands, because glam knows no gender. And of course this is a projection – falling in love is like that. Everything dazzling in the beginning, all perceived qualities bent through a hopeful prism. Whoever knows what Chasing Rainbows is really like except those who said his name like coins dropped into a wishing well?

And if we've learned anything, we've learned that just about everything exists on a spectrum, or in gradients of colour, even the results of my daughter's assessments. Unfortunately, they do not call her sun-kissed, or rainbow child, or anything more connotative of her ability to wield magic after a storm. Chasing Rainbows knew that so many of us desperately wanted to break free from monochrome, not only to see colour – but also feel it and be it. All he sees is colours upon colours upon colours, spectrums inside of spectrums. My blackness is a rainbow and my queerness is a rainbow and my femininity is a rainbow.

If Chasing Rainbows officiates at your wedding, then it's probably a bad omen indicating that either party may wander off looking for something better but in different and independent directions, because rainbows always change their location based on the vantage point of the viewer, like a horizon line or the offing of a sea, the thing that flat earthers don't seem to understand, there is no solid edge to rainbows. They just keep going. They are living in a lucid dream.

What is the Heart of a River

LEISURE

My uncle loved fishing –
as a teen, he'd skip school
and go to the neighbourhood lake,

walk part of the way down
the boardwalk and stand,
like he did when I last saw him,

cast his fishing pole in a flicker,
arced lure, line flying before it dropped
into the belly of Lake Hiawatha.

PUZZLE

As I sit down to do a fact-finding activity
with my daughter, she whizzes through
all the answers she knows and pauses
on a question, *Which is the largest sea creature?*
We circle the 'blue whale'. And I consider its heart.

A blue whale's heart is:
- almost as big as a small piano.
- almost as big as a Harley-Davidson.
- weighs about the same as an oil filled drum.

PULSE

A few times my dad was tasked
with caring for and cleaning
my uncle's L-VAD, which

pumped blood on behalf
of the left chamber of his heart.
A tube reached outside

of my uncle's body and
into a handheld machine.
I can envision them both

in the TV room as dad prepares
the mechanisms, reconnects
the pump of my uncle's heart.

CLOCK

I had a penchant for timepieces,
as though I was a mariner
or a railway conductor at nine.

I wore a pocket watch clasped
to a gold-plated chain with intricate
engravings on the outside, feathers

or raised leaves. The feeling of opening
the case and looking inside, was
the rhythm of a ticking I could both

hear and feel, a 'heart' clasped
to my jeans or shirt pocket – conductor
of my sojourns, mariner of footpaths.

VALVE

What is the heart of a river?

COROLLARY

It could be said that there are three hearts
in 'The Two Fridas' portrait, the two

displayed in the chest of each woman,
but also the closed valve formed by their

enclosed hands, two fists being the size
of an adult human heart, their fingers

like veins on the surface of the muscle,
leading towards and away from each other.

KNOT

Every mammal's heart
develops in the same way. A
blood vessel twists in on itself.

CORRIDOR

Kahlo, with her painting
of hearts and aortic offshoot

wrapped around her lookalike,
both hearts visible through the chest

but one heart opened to reveal
valves and inner chambers;

a vein is attached to the picture
of a former love held by the Kahlo

on the right – which I had thought
was the underside of an areola,

as if Kahlo on the right would
eventually repair Kahlo on the left, but

keep the thin vein and clasped hands
as a connection between them.

She Found God in Herself and She Loved Her Fiercely

My mother said that at five I went to church with a school friend
and saw a large image of a white man on the wall. I couldn't
concentrate on the sermon – my favourite part. That Jesus' whiteness
was so loud, throwing everything out of focus, even God.

My mother doesn't say black people should worship blackness,
but white nativity figures displayed in a black church incites her
to go looking for statuettes with skin the colour of coffee

and hair like lambswool for children to see during praise
and worship. This is her answer to The Doll Tests:
make the church and home sanctuaries for blackness.

Just so she could learn to cut the glass, to make the frame,
to double mat her 24 x 36 inch poster to display
the black Madonna and child in our living room
above the sofa, my mother took a framing job at Michaels.

In one of her posters a man stands guard outside a temple,
his dark skin prominent against marble pillars. He's
so casual in his protective stance that he leans on his staff,
a princely warrior entirely at ease with himself.

When my brother was four, he thought our uncle was Jesus,
confused by our uncle, the pastor's, use of 'I'. My brother
would say, *Remember when Jesus said...* and for a few moments

my mom thought her son was hearing the son of God,
until he began to recount where Jesus had stood –
in the same place as the pastor – speaking with the same voice.

Sudanese Frankincense and Tunisian Myrrh, oils that
– in a similar form – the wise men gave Jesus, were exchanged
in my childhood among women, as if by associating ourselves

with rare and beautiful things, we could relearn to see ourselves
as rare and beautiful. I allow my skin to absorb my mother's
fragrances and musks, high notes of birch wood, base notes of resin.

31

&

I build a shrine: a woman made of clay,
      glazed cerulean blue, her bulbous belly
taut with offspring. She's curled around herself,

ampersand like, red leaves and small notes
      tossed at her feet in gratitude for the belief
child bearing would be painful but smooth,

circuitous but brief, like my birth was – as though
      I had inherited my mother's body along with
the story of her being sent home by the nurses

because she spoke in sentences unbroken by pain.
      She made the circuitous journey to hospital, home,
then back, and delivered me within the hour.

And I am almost ready to forgive the blue figure
      of motherhood for how I birthed, under a heavily
anaesthetized sleep that didn't release me until

the next day, how I was not a witness to my child's
      delivery – its secret – birth occurred to me:
as dream, as void. I was as inert as my mother

was strong, pulled beneath swift currents, and maybe
      this is why I've straddled the pool of motherhood
as if it was a Great Lake, not immersing myself, for fear

of asphyxiation, my limbs bloated with water retention,
      my preemie's lungs not functional yet – we flailed about
on this new shore like fish. I had believed until this point

I was queen of my body, its empress, that I controlled
      its weather if not its forecast, but with the sharp insistence
of scalpels and surgical scissors my body yielded a daughter.

And I am almost willing to curl around a seed of life again,
 to bear its uncomfortable weight, its zombie-like days,
I am almost ready to enter into forgiveness with the same

innocence with which I first entered motherhood,
 believing that nothing untoward could happen to me.

Notes

'The Earth-Eating Fire', Oya is an orisha goddess in the Yoruba religion. 'Cultural burn' is a modern term to describe traditional indigenous practices of creating small-scale fires for a variety of benefits including to safeguard against wildfires. Some sections of this poem are found text from an article on prescribed burning.

'What is the Heart of a River', facts about the blue whale's heart come from the National Geographic.

'She Found God in Herself and She Loved Her Fiercely', the title is an adaptation of a line in Ntozake Shange's choreopoem *For Colored Girls Who Have Considered Suicide/ When the Rainbow is Enuf.* 'The Doll Tests' refer to a psychological study conducted by Doctors Kenneth and Mamie Clark that studied racial perceptions in children.

'Flesh & Tree', was written in response to Oxford University's TIDEfest and Giving Voice workshop with Sarah Howe and Fred D'Aguiar, of which I was an invited participant. The first two stanzas contain descriptions of the salt cellar artefact from Marenka Thompson-Odlum, curator at the Pitt Rivers Museum.

Acknowledgements

My gratitude to the editors of the following publications and commissioning organisations where some of these poems have been published and presented, albeit sometimes in other forms:

Wild Court, Writers Rebel, *Poetry Wales*, *New Voices Rise II*, *The Poetry Review*; *Too Young, Too Loud, Too Different* anthology commemorating twenty years of Malika's Poetry Kitchen. 'Tree Art', originally titled 'Human Ecologies', was commissioned by The Scottish Poetry Library in partnership with Africa in Motion (AiM) Film Festival and Obsidian Foundation. My film *Human Ecologies* debuted at the Africa in Motion Film Festival in 2021 and is available online via The Scottish Poetry Library's website. 'Into the Same Sound Twice', my title poem, was published in *New Humanist*.

Additionally, my profound appreciation to the following individuals and organisations:

For feedback on earlier drafts of these poems and their belief in my work: Dai George, Fiona Sampson, Pascale Petit, Fiona Benson, Prue Bussey-Chamberlain, Lois P James, Peter Hughes and Elena Karina Byrne.

For their mentorship and generosity: Malika Booker, Mimi Khalvati, Roger Robinson, Steve J Fowler.

For supporting my writing development: Poetry London, The London Library, Obsidian Foundation, My Obsidian Group C, Royal Holloway University of London, the Poetry School, The Poetry Review, Jerwood Arts, Writing East Midlands, The Bridge.

For friendship and encouragement: Kendra Williby, Shanita Bigelow, Nikiah Campbell, Jakarra Howard, Reshona Harris, Intisar Abioto, Kalimah Abioto, Esther Kondo Heller, Asmaa Jama, Natalie Linh Bolderston, Leo Boix, Samatar Elmi, Clementine Burnley, Tanatsei Gambura, Ashley Williams-Leon, Luke Kuhns and many others.

For Publication:
I'd like to thank everyone at Seren for their thoughtful dedication to bringing my work out into the world, especially my editors Zoë Brigley and Rhian Edwards. I'd also like to thank my cover artist Angelique Stephenson for her attentiveness to my poems and creating both the front and back covers in response.

I'd like to acknowledge all who have gone before me and made this possible for me.

Love and thanks to my family most of all; my life as a poet began with you.

This book is dedicated to my daughter.